The SONGS of CHRISTMAS

The story of Jesus' birth
Luke 2

Written by Lisa M. Clark

Illustrated by Chris Wold Dyrud

CONCORDIA PUBLISHING HOUSE · SAINT LOUIS

Listen, Mary, do you hear?
　　What a special greeting!
God's dear angel has come near
　　for a holy meeting.
"God's own Son will be your Child;
　　He has shown you favor.
Truly, Mary, young and mild:
　　you will bear the Savior!"

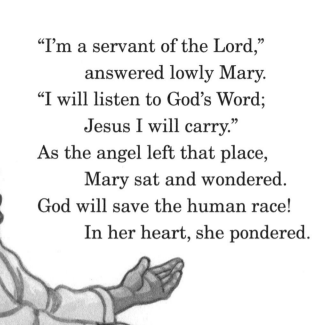

"I'm a servant of the Lord,"
    answered lowly Mary.
"I will listen to God's Word;
    Jesus I will carry."
As the angel left that place,
    Mary sat and wondered.
God will save the human race!
    In her heart, she pondered.

"My soul magnifies the Lord,"
    Mary's voice was singing:
"Let me sing the happy chord!
    Joyful news is ringing!
God's true mercy comes to all,
    even to the lowly.
On His name I humbly call;
    He is truly holy!"

Then the time had come to pass
    for the promised Jesus.
Our Messiah came at last!
    From our sin He frees us!
In the hills outside of town,
    shepherds were unknowing
That God's love was coming down,
    grace to us was showing.

"Hark!" an angel bright appeared.
    "Sleepy shepherds, listen!"
Up they looked with shock and fear;
    heav'nly glory glistened.
Music filled the night just then:
    choirs of angels sharing
Happy news to timid men,
    wondering and staring!

"Peace on earth! All glory be
    to the One who saves you:
God on high eternally—
    His own Son He gave you."
With the dazzling concert done,
    up the shepherds hurried;
Searching for the Promised One,
    into town they scurried.

In a stable, near the hay,
    Mary watched her blessing.
In a manger, Jesus lay
    swaddled up and resting.
As the shepherd men drew near
    to this little treasure,
Quiet humming did they hear
    of a mother's pleasure?

Not long after, Joseph led
    to the temple building;
Doing what the Scriptures said,
    God's own Word fulfilling.
Anna saw the holy Christ
    and gave God the glory
On this day of sacrifice,
    telling all the story.

Praise and singing would not end;
    Simeon was waiting.
He knew that the Lord would send
    cause for celebrating!
"Let Your servant part in peace."
    By the Holy Spirit,
This old man told of God's grace
    to all who would hear it.

"This Child is the Chosen One!
　　　This is God's salvation!
I have seen God's only Son;
　　　He will save the nations!
Mary, I must tell you true;
　　　Songs will turn to crying.
Your heart will start hurting you
　　　when your Son is dying."

Mary didn't understand
    what this man had told her.
Jesus later learned to stand;
    He became much older.
People sang to God in praise
    of a mighty teacher.
Jesus healed and spent His days
    as a faithful preacher.

But one Friday, people killed
    Jesus, our Redeemer.
Joyful tongues and lips were stilled,
    though the earth did tremor.
Silence filled the darkened sky;
    Mary filled with sadness.
But short-lived was time to cry,
    soon would come new gladness!

Easter morning, He arose—
    Jesus is the winner!
Gone are all the tears and woes—
    Free is ev'ry sinner!
Shout with cheering! Raise your voice!
    Spread the Good News story!
We can every day rejoice
    in our Father's glory!

Sing at Christmas without fear—
    Jesus watches o'er you.
Sing at Easter loud and clear—
    He has gone before you.
Up in heaven, Jesus reigns,
    getting all things ready.
We will join in loud refrain,
    voices strong and steady!

Dear Parent,

Christmas is a time full of music and praise in celebration of Jesus' birth. It may surprise some children to know that the Bible is full of songs too. Moses and Miriam sang with the Israelites when they escaped from Egypt. Deborah and King David sang songs of praise after victory. The Book of Psalms is one big songbook!

It shouldn't come as a surprise then that the Bible provides a few songs during the account of Jesus' birth as well. Thousands of years later, the Church still sings the words of praise first given through Mary, the angels, and Simeon.

Christmastime is filled with music, but not all songs point to the gift of our Savior from sin: Jesus, the Son of God. As you sing at church and at home with your family this season, encourage a focus of the real reason for our songs of joy: Jesus came to earth, died for us, and rose again. Because of this, we can someday sing praises forever in the presence of our Lord!

The words of this book are set in a pattern so that they may be sung to the tune of "Gentle Mary Laid Her Child," found on page 374 of *Lutheran Service Book* and in other hymnals as well. Fourteen stanzas is a very long song, so singing the entire book at once may be overwhelming! However, you may choose to sing the book in sections as you prepare for Advent or as you enjoy the Christmas season through Epiphany. However you decide to use this book, may it be a blessing to you and to your family.

The Author